☀ *Creative Education*

BY VALERIE BODDEN

Published by Creative Education
P.O. Box 227, Mankato, Minnesota 56002
Creative Education is an imprint of The Creative Company
www.thecreativecompany.us

Cover design and art direction by Rita Marshall
Interior design and book production by The Design Lab
Printed in the United States of America

Photographs by Alamy (The London Art Archive), Corbis
(Bettmann, Stefano Bianchetti, Leonard de Selva, Hulton-
Deutsch Collection, Scheufler Collection, Underwood
& Underwood), Getty Images (Henry Guttmann, Milos
Oberajger/Topical Press Agency, Time & Life Pictures)

Library of Congress Cataloging-in-Publication Data
Bodden, Valerie.
The assassination of Archduke Ferdinand / by Valerie Bodden.
p. cm. — (Days of change)
Includes bibliographical references and index.
ISBN 978-1-58341-731-7
1. World War, 1914–1918–Causes–Juvenile literature. 2.
World War, 1914–1918–Austria–Juvenile literature. 3. Franz
Ferdinand, Archduke of Austria, 1863–1914–Assassination–
Juvenile literature. I. Title. II. Series.
D512.B63 2009
940.3'11–dc22   2008009162

First Edition
9 8 7 6 5 4 3 2 1

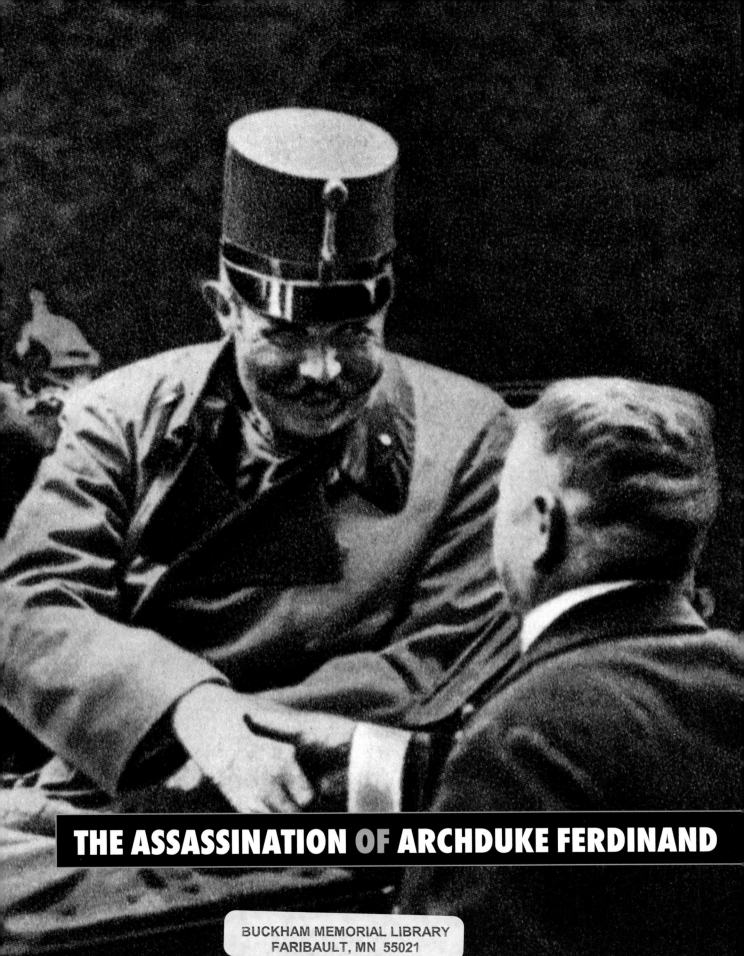

THE ASSASSINATION OF ARCHDUKE FERDINAND

ASSASSINAT DE L'ARCHIDUC HÉRITIER D'AUTRICHE ET DE LA DUCHESSE SA FEMME A SARAJEVO

The shocking murder of Archduke Franz Ferdinand and his wife prompted dramatic illustrations in journals around the world and would soon lead to global repercussions.

Nineteen-year-old

Gavrilo Princip stood brooding outside Schiller's restaurant on the corner of Franz Joseph Street in Sarajevo, Bosnia. It was June 28, 1914, and already that morning, one of his friends had failed in an attempt to assassinate Archduke Franz Ferdinand, heir to the throne of the Austro-Hungarian Empire. Suddenly, Princip saw a large car pull around the corner and stop. Instantly recognizing Franz Ferdinand in the back of the car, Princip pulled out a gun and fired twice. But before he could see if his shots had found their mark, Princip was assailed on all sides and pulled away for questioning.

Princip's bullets had indeed found their target—and as a result, both Franz Ferdinand and his wife Sophie were dead. Exactly one month later, Austria-Hungary responded by declaring war on Serbia, which it claimed had aided in the assassination. Soon, due to a complex web of alliances, many of the world's powers were fighting one another in what came to be known as World War I. By the time it was over, nearly 20 million soldiers and civilians were dead, and people everywhere were asking how a small local spat had turned into a war that engulfed the world.

June 28, 1914

As the people of the world stepped from the 19th century into the 20th, the world was a rapidly changing place. At the dawn of the 1800s, people had traveled by horse, read by candlelight, and talked to one another in person. One hundred years later, people could travel by car, read by the light of an electric bulb, and talk to one another via telephone. This was largely because the Industrial Revolution, a time of great progress in manufacturing techniques, had spread through Europe and the United States during the 18th and 19th centuries, bringing with it rapid development and greater prosperity.

With such progress came a fierce pride among the citizens of many countries in their homeland's achievements. This pride, known as nationalism, led some to believe in the superiority of their own country over the rest of the world. In order to prove that superiority, the world's top powers amassed huge colonial empires, in which a "home" country ruled over the people and resources of other, less powerful nations. These nations were often located far from the motherland.

Most of the world's empires were centered in Europe; Great Britain, France, Germany, the Netherlands, and Portugal all laid claim to colonial possessions overseas. The largest of these empires, that of Great Britain, stretched around the world, from Canada to the Caribbean and from South Africa to India. More than 400 million people—about 25 percent of the world's population—were subject to British rule. Not only was its empire strong, but the British motherland was growing as well.

The early 1900s were a time of rapid advancements in transportation; in America, Henry Ford's Michigan assembly plants turned out popular Model T cars by the thousands.

German Emperor
Wilhelm II

Austro-Hungarian
Emperor Franz Joseph

By 1900, the country's population had reached 37 million, and London was the largest city in the world, with more than 6 million residents. With education and literacy levels growing, newspapers such as the *Daily Mail*—with a million subscribers—found great success.

Even though the German Empire was nowhere near as large as that of Britain, by 1900, the Germans held land in Asia and Africa. More stunning than Germany's colonial possessions, however, was its industrial growth. By the early years of the 20th century, Germany was at the forefront of the electrical and chemical industries. The empire was also a center of European culture, with opera houses, concert halls, and music academies in almost every major city.

To the south of the German Empire lay the Austro-Hungarian Empire, which had been ruled since 1848 by Emperor Franz Joseph, a member of the royal Habsburg family, which had held power in the region since 1282. Covering an area about the size of Texas, Austria-Hungary boasted a population of nearly 50 million. With at least 15 different languages spoken within its borders, the empire included peoples of more than 10 different nationali-

The Staatsoper Hannover, an opera house in the northern German city of Hannover, was the site of many productions that showcased Germany's cultural refinements in the early 1900s.

"*Europe was primed for war [in 1914], and if the assassination [of Franz Ferdinand] by a Slav nationalist had not pitched the world into conflict, . . . then another trigger would probably have done so. . . . The murder of Archduke Ferdinand holds the symbolic power that it does precisely because it acted as catalyst [spark] for the pre-existing currents of political and economic tension, and hurtled the world inexorably [unstoppably] into war. The trends were there, but with hindsight we can say that the world was an utterly different place after Princip pulled the trigger.*"

THE AUSTRALIAN newspaper, 2002

ties, among them Austrians, Germans, Hungarians, Czechs, Poles, Croats, and Italians. The ruling groups in the empire— the Germans of Austria and the Magyars of Hungary—worked hard to hold on to their power. People of royal or noble birth kept a clear separation between themselves and people of "lower" birth, many of whom worked the region's farms.

On the eastern border of Austria-Hungary and Germany lay the enormous Russian Empire, which stretched all the way from eastern Europe and across Asia to the Pacific Ocean. Like Austria-Hungary, Russia was an empire made up of many different nationalities, and more than 100 languages were spoken by its 130 million inhabitants. Although industrialization in coal, iron, and steel production had made Russia the fourth-strongest power in the world, the majority of the empire's citizens were illiterate peasants and unskilled workers who often

Life was hard for many Russians at the dawn of the 1900s; these photos from 1909 show Russian women driving mining carts (top) and carrying water to farm animals (opposite).

faced poverty and hunger. After the government's secret police ordered the massacre of thousands of peaceful demonstrators seeking better working conditions in 1905, people began to call for the revolutionary overthrow of the monarchy.

Meanwhile, across the Pacific, the U.S. was experiencing tremendous growth as immigrants flocked to the "Land of Opportunity." By 1900, the nation's population of 76 million was growing by one million people every year. Nearly one out of every seven people in the young nation was foreign-born. Many immigrants came to the U.S. in search of work, as the country's rapid industrialization had created a demand for laborers. Newly formed companies such as U.S. Steel, Ford Motor Company, and General Motors lured people from rural to urban areas, and soon nearly half of the nation's population was living in cities.

Although the U.S. had few colonies apart from Puerto Rico, Guam, and the Philippines, it was by far the most powerful nation in the Western Hemisphere. The country often used its power and money to influence the nations of Central and South America. America's sway was especially strong in Panama, where the U.S.-administered Panama Canal was completed in 1914 to connect the waters of the Atlantic and Pacific oceans. Other countries, including Argentina, Brazil, and Chile, tried to resist U.S. influence and to develop

American might was on display in Panama in the years before World War I, as the U.S. built
the Panama Canal, improving shipping efficiency in the Americas and the world.

During the early years of the 20th century, the most powerful nations in Europe dedicated themselves to building up their military strength. In every European nation except Britain, all males were required to serve in the military, enabling each country's armed forces to grow huge. In 1912, for example, Germany built up its army to a total force of 665,000 men. In addition to increasing their human resources, the countries of Europe focused on attaining larger and better naval fleets. In 1906, Britain launched the *Dreadnaught* battleship, whose high speed, huge guns, and thick armor made all previous battleships seem weak and useless.

African countries were long claimed as colonies by European powers; this photo shows Spain and France signing a 1912 treaty that gave primary control of Morocco to France.

their own industries. Argentina, for example, was a leading exporter of products such as wool and wheat, and as a result was soon the wealthiest country in Latin America.

While most of Central and South America had won independence from European colonial powers early in the 19th century, many African and Asian nations found themselves under European rule at the start of the 20th century. By 1914, almost all of Africa, apart from Ethiopia, had been taken over by France, Britain, Portugal, Germany, Italy, and Belgium. In Asia, too, colonial powers dominated; only five countries—Afghanistan, China, Japan, Siam (present-day Thailand), and Persia (present-day Iran)—were still independent.

With competition for new colonies—as well as for economic and industrial might—heating up, the nations of Europe soon began to fear one another. In order to strengthen their positions, the most powerful countries began to build up their militaries and form alliances, or military agreements, with one another. By 1907, two major groups had emerged: the Triple Alliance, consisting of Austria-Hungary, Germany, and Italy, and the Triple Entente, made up of Britain, France, and Russia. Because these two major alliances were thought to create a "balance of powers," many in Europe

"There is much agitation throughout the world. The stage is set, the actors are ready. Only the costumes are lacking for the play to begin. The second decade of the twentieth century may witness very grave events. In view of the combustible material about, they may come soon."

BARON ALOIS LEXA VON AEHRENTHAL, Austrian minister of foreign affairs, 1908

15

believed war was unlikely. But events in Europe's flashpoints, such as the Balkans, made some nervous.

The Balkans, a mountainous region at the crossroads of Austria-Hungary, Russia, and the Ottoman Empire (centered in present-day Turkey), was home to several ethnic groups. Greeks, Albanians, Serbs, Croats, Bosnians, Bulgarians, Romanians, and Macedonians all called the area home. Many of these peoples had once been ruled by the Ottoman Empire, but that empire had been pushed out of the Balkans after losing the Russo-Turkish War in 1878. Afterward, some nations, such as Serbia and Montenegro, became independent. The twin provinces of Bosnia and Herzegovina, on the other hand, were given to Austria-Hungary to administer. Then, in 1908, Austria-Hungary decided to annex the two provinces, making them an official part of its territory. Because the majority of Bosnia's population consisted of ethnic Serbs, this move angered neighboring Serbia. Many Serb nationalists there began to feel that it was their duty to free the Serbs living under Austrian rule. Secret terrorist societies, such as the Black Hand, were formed, pledging to unite all the lands that were home to Serbs by any means necessary.

After Serbia gained territory in the Balkans through two local wars,

Gavrilo Princip

This 1908 illustration from the cover of a French journal demonstrates the combustible politics at play in the Balkans, as figures representing the different empires pull at the region.

e Petit Journal

5 CENTIMES **SUPPLÉMENT ILLUSTRÉ** **5** CENTIMES ABONNEMENTS

Le Petit Journal agricole, 5 cent. ～ La Mode du Petit Journal, 10 cent.
Le Petit Journal illustré de la Jeunesse, 10 cent.

On s'abonne sans frais dans tous les bureaux de poste

SIX MOIS
SEINE et SEINE-ET-OISE.. 2 fr.
DÉPARTEMENTS.. .... 2 fr.
ÉTRANGER 2 50

DIMANCHE 18 OCTOBRE 1908   Numér

LE REVEIL DE LA QUESTION D'ORIENT

"[Princip was] undersized, emaciated, sallow, sharp-featured. It was difficult to imagine that so frail-looking an individual could have committed so serious a deed. Even his clear blue eyes, burning and piercing, but serene, had nothing cruel or criminal in the expression."

LEO PFEFFER, investigations judge of Sarajevo district court, 1914

"*If the heir to the throne goes to Bosnia we will see that he pays for it. . . . Serbs, make use of every available weapon, daggers, guns, bombs, and dynamite. Revenge is sacred. Death to the Habsburg dynasty. The memory of those heroes who rise up against it will live forever.*"

SRBOBRAN, Serbian-language newspaper in Chicago, 1913

The son of poor peasants, Gavrilo Princip grew up in a tiny, window-less house in western Bosnia. At the age of 13, he was sent to school in Sarajevo, where he devoured not only the facts he learned in class, but also the revolutionary ideas of the local schoolboys. Soon, he had become an ardent Serb nationalist, and he traveled to Serbia in 1912. There he spent his time with other revolutionaries and attempted to join the Serbian army. Although the small boy was told he was unfit for military service, the rejection did nothing to curb his desire to serve the cause of Serbian nationalism.

officials in Austria-Hungary began to worry. They knew that Serbia wished to unite all Serbs and other South Slavs (Croats, Bosnians, and Slovenes) in a "Greater Serbia" and feared that Serbia would lead the Slavs living in Austria-Hungary to revolt. In an effort to conquer Serbia before this could happen, many Austrian leaders tried to lure their rival into war. But one prominent official opposed war with Serbia: Archduke Franz Ferdinand. Instead, he felt that the best way to prevent a revolt was to give the Serbs in the Austro-Hungarian Empire more say in their government. Unfortunately, he would never get the chance.

Raised in the ways of royalty, Archduke Franz Ferdinand (left) had a passion for history, travel, and hunting.

A bright sun shone in the cloudless sky over the Bosnian capital of Sarajevo on the morning of Sunday, June 28, 1914, as Franz Ferdinand and his wife Sophie prepared to ride through the streets of the city. Usually, Sophie was not allowed to accompany her husband on official imperial business, as she was of "unequal" birth and did not share the rank of her husband. On this day, though, the archduke was

A FATEFUL TRIP

visiting Sarajevo not as the heir to the Austrian throne, but as the inspector-general of the Austrian army, so his wife was allowed to ride by his side.

This was to be the last stop on the couple's four-day visit to Bosnia and Herzegovina. Originally, Franz Ferdinand, knowing that the people of Bosnia were unhappy under Austrian rule, had been reluctant to make the trip. He had even asked his uncle, Emperor Franz Joseph, to excuse him from the assignment, but the emperor's insincere response of "Do as you like" meant not that Franz Ferdinand could opt out of the trip, but that he had to go.

So far, however, the trip had proved uneventful. The inspector-general had been pleased with the 20,000 soldiers he had observed performing military exercises in the rough, mountainous terrain near Sarajevo. His wife, too, had enjoyed her time visiting the schools and orphanages of Sarajevo. The couple had even been greeted with cheers when they had visited the city's marketplace unannounced on the first evening of their trip. In fact, by the evening of June 27, Franz Ferdinand remarked that he was beginning to fall in love with Bosnia. And Sophie cheerfully told a Bosnian politician who

20

Like all members of the Habsburg family, Franz Ferdinand needed the emperor's permission to marry. But when he approached Emperor Franz Joseph with a request to wed Countess Sophie Chotek, Franz Ferdinand was denied. The countess's family was not among the short list of those allowed to marry into the royal line. After much pleading, however, the emperor reluctantly allowed Franz Ferdinand to enter into a morganatic marriage with Sophie. This meant that she could not share his rank and that their children could not inherit the throne. The couple was married on July 1, 1900, and had three children before their deaths in 1914.

Franz Ferdinand met and fell in love with Sophie Chotek at a ball in Prague in 1895; he resolved to marry her, even though it meant his children could never inherit the throne.

had cautioned that the couple's trip to the province would be dangerous that he had been wrong. Even so, the archduke briefly considered skipping the scheduled stop in Sarajevo, as he was eager to get back to his children. After a military aide argued that such a step would offend the citizens of Sarajevo, however, Franz Ferdinand decided that he would stay.

Even as Franz Ferdinand and Sophie were preparing to ride through Sarajevo on the morning of June 28, six young men were taking positions along the route the couple would travel through the city. The course was well-known, as it had been published in the local newspapers so that the residents of Sarajevo could show their loyalty to the crown by lining the streets to cheer as the archduke passed. But these young men weren't there to cheer for the archduke; their mission was to kill the heir, whom

Born on December 18, 1863, Franz Ferdinand was the oldest son of Emperor Franz Joseph's brother, Karl Ludwig. In 1889, the emperor's son, Crown Prince Rudolf, killed himself, making Franz Ferdinand second in line to the throne, after his father. After Karl Ludwig's death in 1896, Franz Ferdinand became the heir to the throne of Austria-Hungary. Although he was devoted to the empire, the archduke wasn't well-liked within the land he was to one day rule. Among everyone but his family, Franz Ferdinand was often cold, aloof, and impatient. At home, though, he was a loving and devoted husband and father who could even be charming at times.

Despite his reputation for being cold and impersonal, Franz Ferdinand was cordial as he greeted Sarajevo citizens with his military aides in the hours before his assassination.

In spite of warnings regarding potential threats against their lives in Sarajevo, both Franz
Ferdinand and Sophie proceeded with the planned motorcade parade through the city.

they saw as a representative of Austrian tyranny. Carrying guns and small bombs filled with nails and lead pieces, the assassins spread out along the Appel Quay, a narrow, winding street along the bank of the sluggish, red-brown Miljačka River, and waited in nervous anticipation for the chance to become Serbian heroes.

Around 10:00 A.M., Franz Ferdinand's seven-car motorcade started along the Appel Quay. In the open-roofed third car sat Franz Ferdinand, dressed in his general's uniform, with a pale blue, high-collared tunic, black pants with red stripes down the sides, and a helmet adorned with green peacock feathers. On his right side was Sophie, wearing a white silk dress encircled by a red sash. Her broad-brimmed hat was ornamented with ostrich feathers.

As the motorcade proceeded slowly through the street, Sarajevo's

25

blend of old mosques and new European buildings gleamed in the baking sunlight. The heat of the day had forced most of the spectators lining the route to seek shade under the trees near the houses and shops on the opposite side of the road from the river. Suddenly, as the archduke's car approached the Cumurja Bridge, a loud crack split the air. Although no one yet realized it, the sound had been made when the safety cap had been popped off a bomb. That bomb now landed on the back of Franz Ferdinand's car and bounced into the street. It exploded on the ground, breaking windows and street lamps, gouging a hole in the road, and injuring several spectators as well as two officers—Count Boos-Waldeck and Lieutenant Colonel Erich von Merizzi—in the car behind the archduke's.

Within moments, the bomb's thrower, 19-year-old Nedeljko Čabrinović, the fourth assassin on the route (the first three had lost their courage as the archduke passed), had jumped into the river. He was quickly pulled out by the police. After seeing that Čabrinović had been apprehended and that the wounded in the car behind his were being tended to, Franz Ferdinand ordered the motorcade to proceed to the town hall.

The cars arrived there without further incident. (The remaining two assassins were unable to take effective aim at the

"If we had known World War I would result, the assassination would not have happened. We didn't think anything like that would be the result; it was the sixth assassination attempt in four years. It was a local affair, a personal affair. We didn't think of the world or of any other country. It was our problem and we were solving it our own way."

CVETKO POPOVIĆ, one of the would-be assassins, 1967

Franz Ferdinand's motorcade traveled Sarajevo streets that were tight, making fast travel difficult in many places and leaving the archduke exposed despite security efforts.

"[Franz Ferdinand] was marvelous as a father to us children. We were always taken with him on every possible occasion, whether traveling, or, when we were old enough, out shooting at home. . . . He was firm with us, but never harsh or unjust. As for those famous tempers that came and went like midsummer storms, we certainly saw him sometimes bang on the table and raise his voice. But it was always with adults, never with us."

SOPHIE NOSTITZ, daughter of Franz Ferdinand and Sophie, 1983

The choice of June 28 as the date for Franz Ferdinand's visit to Sarajevo stirred up feelings of resentment among Serb nationalists. The date was the anniversary of the 1389 Battle of Kosovo Polje, which marked the beginning of the Ottoman takeover of Serbia. Despite the fact that the battle had been fought more than 500 years before, Serbs still honored the day, and many were angered that Franz Ferdinand—who to them represented another oppressor—had chosen that day to visit Sarajevo. It seems unlikely, however, that the date was intentionally chosen by the Austrians, who probably had little knowledge of its significance.

Physically, the city of Sarajevo has long had a strong Islamic character; this street scene displays the domes and minarets of mosques, as well as ornate wooden buildings.

archduke's car since the motorcade was traveling much faster now.) At the town hall, the mayor of Sarajevo launched into his prepared speech, saying, "I consider myself happy that Your Highnesses can read in our faces the feelings of our love and devotion." This was too much for the archduke, who angrily interrupted: "Mr. Mayor, what is the good of your speeches? I come to Sarajevo on a friendly visit and some-one throws a bomb at me. This is outrageous!" After his outburst, Franz Ferdinand let the mayor finish his speech, then read his own pre-pared remarks off a piece of bloodstained paper from the bombed car. At the end, he thanked the people of Sarajevo for their "joy at the failure of the attempt at assassination." Then he headed into the town hall, where he and his staff tried to figure out the safest plan for the rest of the day.

In the end, the archduke decided that he would go to the hospital to visit those who had been wounded in the bombing. General Oskar Potiorek, the gov-ernor of Bosnia and Herzegovina, insisted that a second attack was unlikely. Yet, as an extra precaution, he suggested driving straight back down the Appel Quay and avoiding the streets of the inner city, which the motorcade had originally been sched-uled to travel on the return trip through Sarajevo. The archduke

"We all felt awkward because we knew that when [Franz Ferdinand] went out he would certainly be killed. No, it was not a matter of being told. But we knew how the people felt about him and the Austrians, and we knew that if one man had thrown a bomb and failed, another man would throw another bomb and another after that if he should fail."

Head of Sarajevo's tourist bureau, who was a boy at the town hall ceremony in Sarajevo, 1937

29

agreed. Although Franz Ferdinand requested that Sophie be taken to the governor's mansion, rather than accompany him to the hospital, she insisted on staying by his side.

So, around 10:45 A.M., the archduke and his wife climbed back into their car. This time, Lieutenant Colonel Count Franz Harrach stood on the left running board, serving as a human shield for Franz Ferdinand. When the first two cars in the motorcade mistakenly turned off of the Appel Quay onto Franz Joseph Street, the driver of Franz Ferdinand's car followed. But when General Potiorek, who was also riding in the car, shouted that they were supposed to stay on the quay, the driver stopped the car in order to put it into reverse.

Suddenly, two shots rang out from the right side of the vehicle. At first, no one realized that the archduke and his wife had been hit. Then,

Without a number of coincidences and chance decisions, the assassination of Franz Ferdinand may not have taken place. If the emperor had allowed Franz Ferdinand to forego the trip as requested, he would not have been a target for assassination. Likewise, if the archduke had decided to cancel his trip the night before visiting Sarajevo, he never would have been near the assassins. And, if his driver had gone straight down the Appel Quay, or if Princip had chosen to stand anywhere besides the corner where Franz Ferdinand's car just happened to stop, the young revolutionary wouldn't have had a second chance to kill the heir.

This photograph was taken as Franz Ferdinand and Sophie left the town hall for the hospital; they would be shot and killed five minutes later after their driver made a wrong turn.

Sarajevo police quickly seized Gavrilo Princip after the shots were fired; although Princip was sentenced to 20 years' imprisonment, he would die of tuberculosis just 4 years later.

During the early 20th century, assassination, or political murder, had become almost commonplace, as groups and individuals wanting to draw attention to their causes adopted this drastic measure. From 1900 to 1914, 40 public officials—including U.S. president William McKinley, Italian king Umberto, Serbian king Alexander Obrenovic and Queen Draga, and Mexican president Francisco I. Madero—were killed by assassins. Franz Ferdinand himself had also faced at least three previous assassination attempts. Yet, rather than living in fear, the archduke accepted that assassination was one of the dangers of his position, saying, "Our life is constantly in danger. One has to rely upon God."

blood spurted from Franz Ferdinand's mouth, and Sophie fell over with her head in her husband's lap. As Franz Ferdinand cried out to his wife, telling her to live for their children, the car sped to the governor's mansion, where the two victims, now unconscious, were laid out on beds. The 50-year-old archduke had a bullet through his neck, and his 46-year-old wife had one in her stomach. Both were dead within 15 minutes.

That afternoon, news of the assassination was delivered to Emperor Franz Joseph, who was more shocked than sorrowful over the death of a nephew he had never particularly wanted to see become emperor, largely because of his marriage to a woman of inferior birth. The rest of the world also quickly learned of the shooting, and, in London, the *Daily Chronicle* wrote that the event came "like a clap of thunder to Europe."

34

Despite the *Daily Chronicle*'s ominous prediction, the weeks following the assassination seemed proof that no larger conflict would be sparked by the killings after all. Franz Ferdinand and Sophie were buried together in a vault that Franz Ferdinand had had built at Artstetten Castle in Austria. Although black flags hung on public buildings in the Austrian capital of Vienna, life continued as usual for the empire's inhabitants. Few people mourned the death of the archduke—many hadn't known him, and most of those who did saw him only as "the ogre," a man prone to violent outbursts of temper.

Behind the scenes, however, Austro-Hungarian officials were discussing whether or not to use the assassinations as an excuse to go to war with Serbia. They knew that the assassins (five of whom had been captured shortly after the murders) were from Bosnia and Herzegovina—and were therefore subjects of Austria-Hungary. But they also knew that the assassins had received their weapons from the Black Hand in Serbia. Despite this fact, an Austrian official sent to Serbia found no evidence that the Serbian government itself had been involved in the plot. Yet, many in the Austrian government were still anxious for war.

FROM LOCAL CONFLICT TO WORLD WAR

Austria's ally, Germany, was also eager for war. Many in Germany felt that a European war was unavoidable and that the sooner it occurred, the better it would be for Germany, since Russia, one of the country's main rivals, was growing stronger

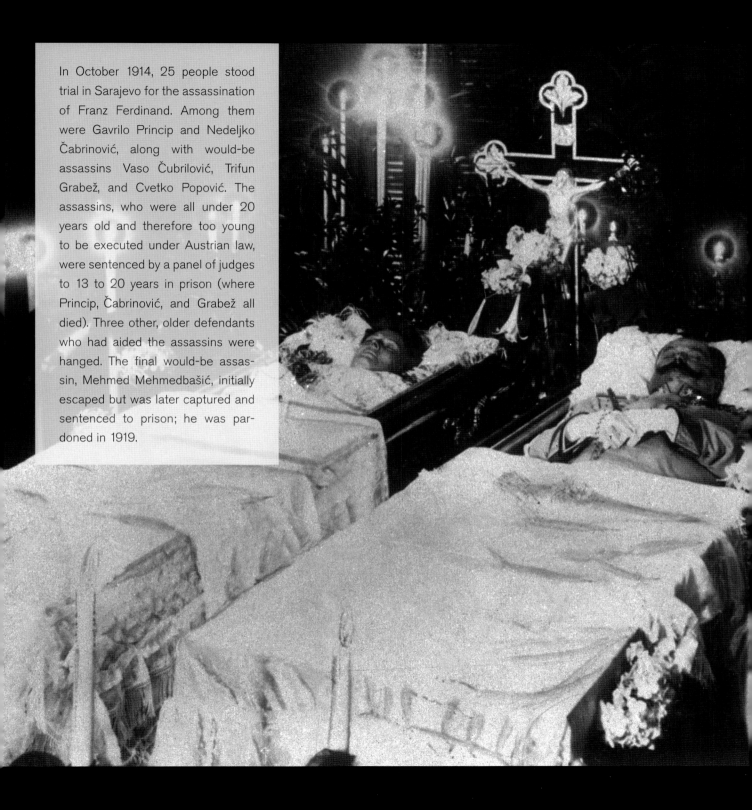

In October 1914, 25 people stood trial in Sarajevo for the assassination of Franz Ferdinand. Among them were Gavrilo Princip and Nedeljko Čabrinović, along with would-be assassins Vaso Čubrilović, Trifun Grabež, and Cvetko Popović. The assassins, who were all under 20 years old and therefore too young to be executed under Austrian law, were sentenced by a panel of judges to 13 to 20 years in prison (where Princip, Čabrinović, and Grabež all died). Three other, older defendants who had aided the assassins were hanged. The final would-be assassin, Mehmed Mehmedbašić, initially escaped but was later captured and sentenced to prison; he was pardoned in 1919.

As Franz Ferdinand and his wife were prepared for burial, Austro-Hungarian officials discussed how they might use the assassinations to their political advantage.

"*This is not the crime of a single fanatic. Assassination represents Serbia's declaration of war on Austria-Hungary. . . . If we miss this occasion, the monarchy will be exposed to new explosions of South Slav, Czech, Russian, Rumanian, and Italian aspirations.*"

GENERAL FRANZ CONRAD VON HÖTZENDORF, Austrian chief of staff, 1914

every year. Thus, shortly after the assassination, Germany offered Austria-Hungary full support should the empire decide to go to war.

Before taking advantage of that support, Austria-Hungary delivered a 10-point ultimatum to Serbia. The ultimatum demanded the breakup of the Black Hand, the censorship of anti-Austrian propaganda, and the tightening of the border between Serbia and Austria-Hungary, among other things. Anxious to avoid war, Serbia agreed to all of the conditions of the ultimatum except one. Serbian officials said they could not allow Austrian officials to participate in the investigation into the assassination, as this would violate the Serbian constitution. Most people believed that such a response meant an end to the threat of war—newspapers in Vienna even declared, "Serbia Accepts Demands, Peace Assured." Officials in Austria-Hungary, though, decided that Serbia's response wasn't good enough, and on July 28, they declared war on Serbia.

"Archduke Franz Ferdinand has been murdered, with his wife, by two Serbs at Sarajevo. What follows from this is not clear. You feel that a stone has begun to roll downhill and that dreadful things may be in store for Europe. I am proposing on 1 October to start my military service. . . . I'm twenty, you see, a fine age for soldiering, I don't know a better."

HERBERT SULZBACH, German citizen, June 28, 1914

37

In response, Serbian ally Russia began to mobilize, or ready its troops, which led Germany to mobilize and declare war on Russia on August 1. France, which had a treaty with Russia, then began to mobilize, and Germany declared war

After Franz Ferdinand's killing, Germany mobilized for war; this photo shows a German officer putting up a sign announcing the country's declaration of war against Russia.

on the French on August 3. The next day, German troops moved into neutral Belgium on their way to France. In response, Britain, which had signed a treaty pledging to protect Belgium's neutrality, declared war on Germany. Over the following days and months, other nations, such as Italy and Japan, joined the fight on the side of the Allies (Serbia, Britain, France, and Russia). The Ottoman Empire and Bulgaria entered the fray on the side of the Central Powers (Austria-Hungary and Germany).

In a burst of patriotism, people in the countries involved in the war hurried to join the armed forces. Many looked at war as a chance to escape their boring, everyday lives and win glory for themselves. Most thought that the war would be short-lived; British soldiers looked forward to returning home victorious by Christmas.

As Great Britain entered the war to uphold its treaty with Belgium, men responded to posters proclaiming "Your King and Country Need You" by reporting to recruiting stations.

In an image that reveals the horror and monotonous devastation of trench warfare, weary French soldiers stand among mangled corpses in a standoff with Germans in similar trenches.

But the reality of the "Great War" was much different. By Christmas, rather than being over, the war was at a stalemate, especially on the western front (mainly in France). Both sides engaged in a new kind of fighting called trench warfare, in which soldiers spent most of their time huddled in deep, barbed-wire-protected ditches in the ground. When they wanted to attack their opponents, they went "over the top," or out of the trenches, and made a mad dash for their enemy's trenches, as soldiers on the other side sprayed machine-gun fire at them. Rather than bringing glory to soldiers, such fighting brought only blood and death.

Although the U.S. tried to remain isolated from what it considered a European war, America joined the fight on the side of the Allies in April 1917 after intercepting a German message promising Mexico U.S. land if it joined the Central Powers. With the

42

U.S. entrance into the war, the Allies finally began to make some headway against the Central Powers, who requested an armistice on November 8, 1918. Three days later, the war was over.

Although people around the world were relieved that the war had finally come to an end, there was little to celebrate. More than 10 million soldiers had died, and another 20 million were wounded. In addition, at least 7 million civilians had been killed during the war, and up to 21 million more died immediately afterward as an influenza epidemic spread across Europe's devastated landscape.

Those who survived the war and the flu epidemic were confronted with a whole new world order. In the Allied nation of Russia, which had been forced to surrender to the Central Powers in March 1918, heavy war losses had helped lead to the overthrow of the monarchy. In its place, a new Communist government (in which all land and businesses were owned by the government) soon emerged. Although Britain and France had experienced victory in the war, both were exhausted and nearly bankrupt by the time the fighting ended, and they lost their positions as world powers. In their place, the U.S. emerged as the wealthiest and most powerful country in the world.

The Central Powers fared much worse. The Austro-Hungarian Empire fell apart before the end of the war, and the Ottoman Empire followed soon after. With the end of hostilities,

After World War I, the Allies were determined that never should another global war devastate the lives of people around the world. As a step toward maintaining peace, the League of Nations, an alliance of countries dedicated to preventing war through negotiation and diplomacy, was formed. Although the League was originally proposed by U.S. president Woodrow Wilson, the U.S. never became a member of the organization. Without U.S. backing, and with no good way to enforce its decrees, the League of Nations proved unsuccessful in preventing World War II. After that conflict, the League was disbanded, and in its place rose the United Nations.

While the end of World War I was cause for celebration, many towns and villages—such as Thiaucourt, France—were left in ruins after the Allies drove the Central Powers back.

the Allies drew up a new map of the region. Austria and Hungary were separated, and the new nations of Finland, Estonia, Latvia, Lithuania, Poland, and Czechoslovakia were created. In the Balkans, Serbs, Croats, and Slovenes from Serbia, Bosnia, and other states were merged into a new country called Yugoslavia. Despite the fact that they were free from Austrian and Ottoman rule, the various groups in the new country continued to fight. In the early 1990s, Yugoslavia broke apart, leaving in its place several smaller countries, including Slovenia, Croatia, Macedonia, Bosnia and Herzegovina, and Serbia. Even today, ethnic tensions continue to rock this region of the world.

In Germany, too, the consequences of the war were severe.

"I am not a criminal, for I have removed an evildoer. I meant to do a good deed."

GAVRILO PRINCIP, assassin of Archduke Franz Ferdinand, 1914

At the peace conference held in Versailles, France, in 1919, the Allies claimed that Germany bore the brunt of the guilt for the war. They argued that the Germans had turned a dispute between Austria-Hungary and Serbia into a worldwide conflict and had caused most of the damage to western Europe during the course of that conflict. Through the Treaty of Versailles, the Germans were forced to accept responsibility for the war and to pay $33 billion to the Allies. Although they signed the treaty, the Germans resented its harsh terms and longed for revenge.

44

Only 20 years after what many had hoped would be the "war to end all wars," Germany would seek that revenge through World War II.

With consequences of such magnitude credited to World War I, historians have long debated what truly caused the war. Some insist that because of the European system of imperialism, rivalries, and alliances, war was inevitable. They say that if it hadn't been sparked by the assassination of Franz Ferdinand, it would have been set off by some other event. Others say that until 1914, the balance of power in Europe had actually prevented war on a number of occasions. They point to the assassination as the direct cause of the war. Whether the assassination caused the war or was simply the occasion for it, though, one thing is certain: it marked a turning point in world history.

Today, Bosnia and Herzegovina is a single, independent nation, but the country's independence did not come without cost. After the breakup of Yugoslavia in the 1990s, Bosnia was the site of bitter conflict, as the nation's different groups—Muslims, Croats, and Serbs—vied for control. During the fighting, thousands of non-Serbs were killed in a policy known as "ethnic cleansing." Ultimately, the North Atlantic Treaty Organization (NATO), an alliance of the U.S. and European countries, intervened. In November 1995, the Dayton peace accord finally brought an end to the fighting by separating Bosnia into two states: the Federation of Bosnia and Herzegovina and the Serb Republic.

Germany's defeat in World War I left the country politically unstable; it took on a communist government briefly in 1919 and would later became fascist under Adolf Hitler.

BIBLIOGRAPHY

Brook-Shepherd, Gordon. *Archduke of Sarajevo: The Romance & Tragedy of Franz Ferdinand of Austria*. Boston: Little, Brown and Company, 1984.

Cassels, Lavender. *The Archduke and the Assassin: Sarajevo, June 28th 1914*. New York: Stein and Day, 1984.

Feuerlicht, Roberta Strauss. *The Desperate Act: The Assassination of Franz Ferdinand at Sarajevo*. New York: McGraw-Hill, 1968.

Fleming, D. F. *The Origins and Legacies of World War I*. Garden City, N.Y.: Doubleday, 1968.

Joll, James. *The Origins of the First World War*. New York: Longman, 1984.

Pauli, Hertha. *The Secret of Sarajevo: Franz Ferdinand, Sophie and the Assassination that Led to World War I*. New York: Appleton-Century, 1965.

Remak, Joachim. *The Origins of World War I, 1871–1914*. New York: Holt, Rinehart and Winston, 1967.

INDEX